A CUP OF TEA
AND A PROVERB

Exploring the Proverbs while enjoying your favorite cup of tea and reaping mental, spiritual, and physical health each day!

Enjoy the journey over the next 31 days!

ACKNOWLEDGEMENTS

Ephesians 3:20 Now unto Him who by the power of work within us is able to accomplish abundantly far more than all we can ask or imagine, to him be glory in the church and in Christ Jesus to all generations, forever and ever, amen.

Special Thank You:

To my husband, Pastor Ron Woods, thank you for your encouragement throughout this process. Thank you for the weekends away to work on this assignment.

To my son Alex Woods who has a gift of exhortation that's amazing. Thank you for encouraging me to persevere and finish this assignment.

To my cousin Nichole Bethel who supported me with this assignment in a major way.

To my circle of friends and everyone who prayed me through this assignment.

ABOUT THE AUTHOR

Kelli Woods is a wife, mother, educator, author and Biblical Counselor.

Kelli has been married to Pastor Ron Woods for 23 years. Their son, Alex, is 22 years old. Kelli has been an educator for over 25 years and she has been a certified Biblical Counselor for 22 years.

Kelli also has a certificate in Theology and Ministry. She has used her strengths in teaching, leading and counseling to minister to and encourage many.

All women need strong relationships to sustain them. However, as women we are often so busy with family, work, and various other responsibilities that the one relationship that often goes forgotten in the craziness of every day life, which is the most important of all, is our relationship with God.

As you read through this devotional, I pray that you commit to setting aside time to relax, be quiet and be still. This special time will be the most important part of your day, if you allow God to quench your thirst.

Tea revives, comforts, warms and relaxes us all at the same time. A hearty cup of tea along with spending time with God can really rejuvinate us. It is my prayer that, as you journey through each Proverb daily, in this devotional, while sipping on your favorite cup of tea, you will be drawn into a more intimate relationship with God.

YOU HAVE A CHOICE!

Verses 5,7

A wise man will hear and increase in learning. Fools despise wisdom and instruction.

What a contrast. What is the difference between a wise man and a fool according to the Bible? Today we will explore Proverbs for the answer to this question.

A wise man	vs	A foolish man

A wise man

→ Proverbs 2:6 receives wisdom from the Lord.
→ Proverbs 2:11 is discrete.
→ Proverbs 2:12 is delivered from the way of Evil.
→ Proverbs 3:14 has proceeds that are Better than profits of silver.
→ Proverbs 3:16 has long life.
→ Proverbs 3:17 has peace.
→ Proverbs 9:8 will love you when he Is rebuked.
→ Proverbs 9:9 will increase in learning.
→ Proverbs 10:8 receives commands.
→ Proverbs 10:19 restrains his lips.
→ Proverbs 11:30 wins souls.
→ Proverbs 12:18 tongue promotes health.
→ Proverbs 12:15 heads counsel.
→ Proverbs 16:23 his heart teaches his Mouth and adds learning to his Lips.
→ Proverbs 21:11 when he is instructed receives knowledge.

A foolish man

→ Proverbs 11:7 Despises wisdom and instruction.
→ Proverbs 1:22 hates knowledge.
→ Proverbs 1:32 is complacent.
→ Proverbs 10:17 spreads slander.
→ Proverbs 10:23 doing evil is a sport to the foolish man.
→ Proverbs 11:29 will be a servant to the wise.
→ Proverbs 12:15 is right in his own eyes.
→ Proverbs 12:23 heart proclaims foolishness.
→ Proverbs 13:19 will not depart from evil.
→ Proverbs 14:9 mocks at sin.
→ Proverbs 14:16 rages and is self-confident.
→ Proverbs 15:5 despises instruction.
→ Proverbs 15:2 mouth feeds on foolishness.
→ Proverbs 18:2 Has no delight in understanding, but in expressing his own heart.

REFLECTION

1. Which of the two best describe you?
2. In what ways do you demonstrate wisdom? In what ways do you represent the fool according to the Bible?
3. How can you gain more wisdom?
4. In every interaction today think about whether you are being wise or foolish.
5. Remember James 1:5 If any of you is lacking wisdom, ask God, who gives to all generously, and it will be given to you.

TEA:

As you explore today's Proverb why not take it all in while sipping on a cup of Blackberry Sage tea. Some of the great benefits of drinking **Blackberry Sage Tea** are:

→ It's considered a tea to drink for wisdom.
→ It contains high levels of anti-oxidants.
→ It helps with many illnesses and digestive disorders (diarrhea, stomach bloating and discomfort.)
→ It stimulates cognitive function.
→ It is used to treat ulcers.

enJOY!

ARE YOU LISTENING TO WHAT GOD IS SAYING?

Verses 2,6 Incline your ears to wisdom. For the Lord gives wisdom.

Today as we explore Proverbs 2 answer the question...... Are you listening to God?

Consider every verse and interpret how it speaks to you personally.

I Samuel 3:10 Now the Lord came and stood there, calling as before, "Samuel! Samuel!" And Samuel said, "Speak, for your servant is listening."

John 10:27 My sheep hear my voice, and I know them and they follow Me.

Luke 11:28 But He said, More than that, "Blessed are those who hear the word of God and keep it."

James 1:19 So then, my beloved brethren, let every man be swift to hear, slow to speak, slow to wrath;

James 1:22 But be doers of the word, and not hearers only, deceiving yourselves.

Proverb 16: 20 He who heeds the word wisely will find good, And whoever trusts in the Lord, happy is he.

Matthew 7:24 Therefore whoever hears these sayings of Mine, and does them, I will liken him to a wise man who built his house on a rock:

Matthew 4:4 But, He answered and said, "It is written, Man shall not live by bread alone, but by every word that proceeds from the mouth of God."

Philippians 4:9 The things which you learned and received and heard and saw in me, these do, and the God of peace will be with you.

Malachi 2:2 If you will not hear, And if you will not take to heart, To give glory to my name," says the Lord of hosts, " I will send a curse upon you, And I will curse your blessings. Yes, I have cursed them already, because you do not take it to heart.

Proverb 19:20 Listen to counsel and receive instruction, That you may be wise in your latter days.

Proverb 5:7 Therefore hear me now, my children, And do not depart from the words of My mouth.

Proverb 7:24 Now therefore, listen to me, my children; Pay attention to the words of my mouth:

Proverb 8:32-35 "Now therefore, listen to me, my children, For blessed are those who keep my ways. Hear instruction and be wise, And do not disdain it, Blessed is the man who listens to Me, watching daily at my gates, Waiting at the posts of my doors. For whoever finds Me finds life, And obtains favor from the Lord;

Proverb 15:31 The ear that hears the rebukes of life will abide among the wise.

REFLECTION:

1. List some of the things that God has been saying to you. Have you been responding in obedience to Him?
2. What is the difference between hearing and listening? Have you been hearing God or listening to Him?
3. How has the above verses given you a clearer perspective of listening verses hearing?
4. Today as God speaks to you write down everything He says.
5. Select the most poignant verse and this week commit it to memory.

TEA:

As you explore today's Proverb why not take it all in while sipping on a cup of **Oolong Tea**. Some of the great benefits of drinking **Oolong Tea** are:

→ Boosts your metabolism

→ Lowers cholesterol

→ Increases mental alertness

→ Aids digestion

→ Promotes healthy hair

→ Betters your skin condition

→ Stabilizes your blood sugar

→ Prevents tooth decay

→ Strengthens immune system

enJOY!

WHO HAS THE LORD SENT YOUR WAY?

Verses 27-29 (The Message)

Never walk away from someone who deserves help; your hand is God's hand for that person. Don't tell your neighbor "maybe some other time" or "try me tomorrow" when the money is right there in your pocket.

Like it or not as Christians we represent Jesus in all that we do.

As we look at today's scripture we are reminded that every day we are given an opportunity to Do good to others.

Romans 12:1 remind us that we are to present our bodies as a living sacrifice.

Philippians 2:3 remind us to esteem others above ourselves. Philippians 2:4 reminds us to

Not only look out for our own interests but we should also look out for the interests of others. I will reiterate, every day the Lord gives us some opportunity to be a blessing to others in need. As Christians we are blessed to be a blessing to others.

We have to be intentional about looking for opportunities to show off Jesus by being a blessing to others.

Today as we explore Proverbs 3 consider what the Word of God has to say about verses 27-29.

Proverbs 11:25 The generous soul will be made rich, and he who waters will also be watered himself.

II Corinthians 9:8-11 And God is able to make all grace abound toward you, that you, always having all sufficiency in all things may have an abundance for every good work. As it is written: He has dispersed abroad, He has given to the poor; His righteousness endures forever.

Now may He who supplies seed to the sower, and bread for food, supply and multiply the seed you have sown and increase the fruits of your righteousness, while you are enriched in everything for all liberality, which causes thanksgiving through us to God.

II Corinthians 9:6 But this I say: He who sows sparingly will also reap sparingly, and He who sows bountifully will also reap bountifully.

Matthew 7:12 Therefore, whatever you want men to do to you, do also to them, For this is the law and the Prophets.

REFLECTION:

1. How well are you representing the Lord?
2. How often do you cease the moment when given the opportunity to be a blessing to someone in need?
3. Are you looking for opportunities to come your way?
4. How has each of the above verses spoken personally to you? Journal your answers.
5. Be intentional about being a blessing today!

TEA:

As you explore today's Proverb why not take it all in while sipping on a cup of **Blueberry Tea**. Some of the great benefits of drinking **Blueberry Tea** are:

→ Supplies antioxidants
→ Reduces the risk of diabetes
→ Full of vitamin C
→ Boosts the immune system
→ Prevents dehydration

enJOY!

HELP LORD! I AM HAVING A HEART ATTACK!

Verse 23 *Keep your heart with all diligence for out of it springs the issues of life.*

In a natural sense the heart is the organ that pumps blood throughout the entire body through the circulatory system, supplying oxygen and nutrients to the tissues and removing carbon dioxide and other waste.

Maintaining an unhealthy lifestyle can contribute to having a heart attack (an improper diet; not exercising regularly etc.). A heart attack in a natural sense can occur by blockage or hardening of the arteries caused by a buildup of plaque.

Plaque in the arteries is dangerous because it can block the flow of blood to the heart, either partially or completely. It is said that heart disease is a silent killer.

In a spiritual sense not spending quality time in prayer, not spending time hearing from God, not spending time reading God's Word, fasting (not making all spiritual disciplines a priority) can lead to a spiritual heart attack and like a natural heart attack become a silent killer.

Bitterness, anger, unforgiveness, envy, jealousy, adultery, fornication, lust, idolatry, selfish ambitions, covetousness just to name a few are those sins that cause blockage. Unchecked they can contribute to having a spiritual heart attack, a heart no longer longing after God, a hardened heart.

Mark 7:15, 21-23 There is nothing that enters a man from outside which can defile him, but the things that come out of him, those are the things that defile a man.

For from within, out of the heart of man, proceed evil thoughts, adulteries, fornications, murders, thefts, covetousness, wickedness, deceit, lewdness, an evil eye, blasphemy, pride, foolishness: All these things come from within and defile a man.

Luke 6:45 A good man out of the good treasure of his hear brings forth good; and an evil man out of the evil treasure of his heart brings forth evil. For out of the abundance of the heart his mouth speaks.

REFLECTION:

1. Are you avoiding a spiritual heart attack?
2. What are some of the things that you are engaged in that is causing poor spiritual health and what are you willing to do to become more spiritually healthy?
3. What can you do to maintain good spiritual heart health?
4. Who are you accountable to for periodic check- ups as it pertains to your spiritual health? Proverbs 27:17; James 5:16
5. Check your spiritual heart health regularly.

TEA:

As you explore today's Proverb why not take it all in while sipping on a cup of **Green Tea**. Some of the great benefits of drinking **Green Tea** are:

→ Good for weight loss
→ Helps regulate glucose levels
→ Improves dental health
→ Improves cholesterol levels
→ Reduces the risk of high blood pressure
→ Reduces risks of neurological disorders

enJOY!

"EL ROI- HE SEES"

Verse 21 For the ways of man are before the eyes of the Lord, And He ponders all his paths.

Today's verse in Proverbs 5 reminds me of Hagar in Genesis 16. Sarai, Abrams wife, could not have children. Sarai convinced Abram to sleep with her maidservant Hagar. Abram listened and slept with Hagar and Hagar conceived. Sarai then despised Hagar and began treating her harshly. Hagar ran away, into the wilderness, from Sarai because of the unfair and harsh treatment.

The angel of the Lord spoke to Hagar in the wilderness asking her where she came from and where she was going. She replied, "running from Sarai." The angel of the Lord told Hagar to return and submit to Sarai and reminded her that the Lord heard her affliction. Hagar then called the Lord El-Roi - You are the God who sees.

What an awesome illustration of how God sees every detail of our lives and as His children we can trust that He is going to work everything out for our good and His glory. We are also reminded of that in Psalm 139:1-11 *O Lord, You have searched me and known me. You know my sitting down and my rising up; You understand my thought afar off. You comprehend my path and my lying down, And are acquainted with all my ways. For there is not a word on my tongue, But behold, O Lord, You know it altogether. You have hedged me behind and before, And laid Your hand upon me. Such knowledge is too wonderful for me; It is high, I cannot attain it. Where can I go from Your Spirit? Or where can I flee from Your presence? If I ascend into heaven, you are there; If I make my bed in hell, behold, You are there. If I take the wings of the morning, And dwell in the uttermost parts of the sea, Even there Your hand shall lead me, And Your right hand shall hold me. If I say "Surely the darkness shall fall on me," Even the night shall be light about me;*

REFLECTION:

1. Read the entire Psalm 139. Make every verse personal for you.
2. Write a summary of how this Psalm spoke to you.
3. When life presents obstacles and challenges, do you really trust that God is El-Roi? Why/Why not?
4. Are you convinced that the ways of man are before the eyes of the Lord, And He ponders all his paths? Explain.
5. List a situation in your past when you had the opportunity to experience God as El-Roi. Remember He is the same God yesterday, today and forevermore.

REMEMBER in every one of life's circumstances even in those times where it just does not seem like He's present- He is El-Roi. He sees it all! Hallelujah!!!

TEA:

As you explore today's Proverb why not take it all in while sipping on a cup of **White Tea**. Some of the great benefits of drinking **White Tea** are:

→ contains antioxidants
→ contains fluoride
→ can accelerate metabolism
→ May be beneficial in preventing cancer
→ Helps lower blood pressure
→ Helps lower cholesterol
→ Reduces blood sugar
→ Helps kill bacteria and viruses

enJOY!

GOD HATES SIN!

Verses 16-19 These six things the Lord hates, Yes seven that are an abomination to Him: A proud look, A lying tongue, Hands that shed innocent blood, A heart that devises wicked plans, feet that are swift in running to evil, A false witness who speaks lies, And one who sows discord among brethren.

As Christians we are made after the image of God. Therefore, we should hate what God hates. Today we will let God's word speak for itself as we take a look at various scriptures.

Pride	Lying	Wickedness
Isaiah 2:12	Proverbs 19:19	Ephesians 5:11
Proverb 8:13	Proverbs 12:22	Ephesians 6:12
Proverbs 11:2	Psalm 107:7	Ecclesiastes 12:14
Proverb 13:10	Colossians 3:9,10	Psalms 5:4
Proverbs 29:23	Proverbs 12:19	Proverbs15:21
Proverbs 18:12	Proverbs 19:5	I Thessalonians 5:22

Evil	Division
Psalm 34:16	Romans 16:17,18
Isaiah 31:2	I Corinthians 1:10-13
Micah 2:1	I Corinthians 3:3
I Corinthians 10:21	I Corinthians 6:1
Proverbs 22:8	I Corinthians 11:18
Psalms 37:9	Luke 11:17

REFLECTION:

1. Which verses spoke directly to you? Write them out. Memorize them.
2. Are there some changes that need to be made in your life as a result? Write them down.
3. What will you do different starting today?
4. Do you have an accountability partner to share these things with? Are you willing to ask that person to really hold you accountable as you seek to please the Lord even more?
5. Yes, God loves you and yet He hates sin. Why does God hate sin? Something to ponder.

TEA:

As you explore today's Proverb, why not take it all in while sipping on a cup of **Matcha Green Tea**. Some of the great benefits of drinking **Match Green Tea** are:

→ Rich in fiber
→ Lowers blood pressure
→ Lowers cholesterol
→ Lowers blood sugar
→ Calms and relaxes
→ Aids in concentration
→ Fights against viruses and bacteria

enJOY!

HUPAKOU

Hupakou - Greek for *Listen attentively* (actively following a command)

Verse 2 *Keep my commands and live, And my law as the apple of your eye.*

I Samuel15:22 So Samuel said: "Has the Lord as great delight in burnt offerings and sacrifices, As in obeying the voice of the Lord? Behold, to obey is better than sacrifice, And to heed than the fat of rams.

We say this verse. We may know this verse. We may even go as far as memorizing this verse, but do we really live by this verse? As we look at today's verse in Proverbs 7:2 it really speaks to how imperative it is that we live a life of obedience. So many Christians "know" the word of God. It is one thing to "know" the scriptures. It is another thing completely to live them. (Colossians 3:16 Let the word dwell in you richly.)

Today let's look at what the Bible has to say about keeping God's commands living out obedience. Let's strive to be obedient the first time. "Keep my commandments and live."

John 8:51 Most assuredly, I say to you, if anyone keeps My word he shall never see death.

Deuteronomy 28:1 Now it shall come to pass, if you diligently obey the voice of the Lord your God, to observe carefully all His commands which I command you today, that the Lord your God will set you high above all nations of the earth.

Deuteronomy 5:33 You shall walk in all the ways which the Lord your God has commanded you, that you may live and that it may be well with you, and that you may prolong your days in the land which you shall possess..

Joshua 1:8 This Book of the law shall not depart from your mouth, but you shall meditate in it day and night, that you may observe to do according to all that is written in it. For then you will make your way prosperous, and then you will have good success.

Malachi 2:2 If you will not hear, And if you will not take it to heart, To give glory to My name, "Says the Lord of hosts", I will send a curse upon you, And I will curse your blessings. Yes, I have cursed them already, Because you don't take it to heart.

I Kings 2:3 And keep the charge of the Lord your God: to keep His statutes, His commandments, His judgments, and His testimonies, as it is written in the Law of Moses, that you may prosper in all that you do and wherever you turn;

Luke 11:28 But He said, "More than that, blessed are those who hear the word and keep it!"

John 14:15 If you love Me, keep My commandments.

Deuteronomy 11:1 "Therefore you shall love the Lord your God, and keep His charge, and His commandments always.

I John 5:3 For this is the love of God, that we keep His commandments. And His commandments are not burdensome.

Luke 6:46 But why do you call me "Lord, Lord" and not do the things which I say?

II Chronicles 3:21 And in every work that he began in the service of the house of God, in the law and in the commandment, to seek his God, he did it with all his heart. So he prospered.

Jeremiah 7:23 But this is what I command them, saying, "Obey My voice and I will be your God, and you shall be My people. And walk in all the ways that I have commanded you, that it may be well with you."

Psalm 119: 104 Through Your precepts I get understanding; Therefore I hate every false way.

Proverbs 13:13 He who despises the word will be destroyed, But he who fears the commandment will be rewarded.

Deuteronomy 4:1 Now, O Israel, listen to the statutes and the judgments which I teach you to observe, that you may live, and go in and possess the land which the Lord God of your fathers is giving you.

II John 1:6 This is love, that we walk according to His commandments. This is the commandment, that as you have heard from the beginning, you should walk in it.

Of course the word of God is loaded with scriptures on obedience I just wanted to share a few.

REFLECTION:

1. Which verse/verses challenged you the most to walk in obedience to God? What are you going to do about it?
2. Which area of your life have you consciously been disobedient to God? Are you willing to repent now? What will you do differently?
3. Name one thing that you know that the Lord has been calling you to do and you have not done it even up to this point? When will you begin?
4. Do you realize that your disobedience could be hindering someone else's blessing?
5. How does I Samuel 5:22 speak to you (obedience is better than sacrifice)?

 ## TEA:

As you explore today's Proverb why not take it all in while sipping on a cup of **Hibiscus Tea**. Some of the great benefits of drinking **Hibiscus Tea** are:

→ Contains vitamin C
→ Lowers blood pressure
→ Lowers cholesterol
→ Protects the liver
→ It has some anti-cancer properties
→ Good for menstrual pain
→ Aids in digestion
→ Beneficial for weight loss
→ May reduce anxiety and depression

enJOY!

A HEART OF HUMILITY

Verse 13 *The fear of the Lord is to hate evil; Pride and arrogance and the evil way And the perverse mouth I hate.*

Hate, we all know, is a very strong word. Today's verse speaks of things that the Lord hates. All of them are rooted in pride. How do you conquer pride and arrogance? Ask the Lord to give you a heart of humility. The ultimate picture of humility is found in John 13:3-17.

Jesus, knowing that the Father had given all things into His hands, and that He had come from God and was going to God, rose from supper and laid aside His garments, took a towel and girded Himself. After that, He poured water into a basin and began to wash the disciples' feet, and to wipe them with the towel with which He was girded. Then He came to Simon Peter. And Peter said to Him, "Lord, are you washing my feet?" Jesus answered and said to him "What I am doing you do not understand now, but you will know after this." Peter said to Him, "You shall never wash my feet!" Jesus answered him, "If I do not wash you, you have no part with Me." Simon Peter said to Him" Lord, not my feet only, but also my hands and my head!" Jesus said to him,"He who is bathed needs only to wash his feet, but is completely clean; and you are clean, but not all of you."

For He knew who would betray Him; therefore He said, "You are not all clean." So when He had washed their feet, taken His garments, and sat down again, He said to them, "Do you know what I have done to you? You call Me Teacher and Lord, and you say well, for so I am. If I then, your Lord and Teacher, have washed your feet, you also ought to wash one another's feet. For I have given you an example, that you should do as I have done to you. Most assuredly I say to you, a servant is not greater than his master; nor is he who is sent greater than he who sent him. If you know these things, blessed are you if you do them."

Today I share with you some other scriptures to help develop a heart of humility.

Ephesians 4:2 with all lowliness and gentleness, with longsuffering, bearing with one another in love.

Romans 12: 16 Be of the same mind toward one another. Do not set your mind on high things, but associate with the humble. Do not be wise in your own opinion.

Proverbs 11:2 When pride comes, then comes shame; But with the humble is wisdom.

James 4:10 Humble yourself in the sight of the Lord, and He will lift you up.

Colossians 3:12 Therefore, as the elect of God, holy and beloved, put on tender mercies, kindness, humility, meekness, longsuffering;

Poverbs 22:4 By humility and the fear of the Lord are riches and honor and life.

Proverbs 18:12 Before destruction the heart of man is haughty, and before honor is humility.

Mark 9:35 And He sat down, called the twelve, and said to them," If anyone desires to be first, he shall be last of all and servant of all.

Luke 14:11 For whoever exalts himself will be humbled, and he who humbles himself will be exalted.

II Corinthians 11:30 If I must boast, I will boast in the things which concern my infirmity.

Daniel 4:37 Now I, Nebuchadnezzar, praise and extol and honor the King of heaven, all of whose works are truth, and His ways justice. And those who walk in pride He is able to put down.

Pride is a natural part of who we are. We have to be persistent and intentional about daily asking the Lord to give us a heart of humility.

REFLECTION:

1. As you ponder today's verse in Proverbs 8, consider what it means to fear the Lord?

2. Are you a servant at heart? Explain.

3. If you would be honest and true to yourself do you struggle with pride? Are you willing to allow the Lord to work on your heart that you may more consistently walk in humility?

4. What does it mean to "put on humility" as commanded in Colossians 3:12?

5. Why do you think God hates pride?

 TEA:

As you explore today's Proverb why not take it all in while sipping on a cup of **Lemongrass Tea**. Some of the great benefits of drinking **Lemongrass Tea** are:

→ Helps digestion
→ Helps reduce cholesterol
→ Cleanses and detoxifies
→ Heals cold and flu
→ Helps fight cancer
→ Reduces arthritis pain
→ Helps fight depression
→ Helps keep skin healthy

enJOY!

"OUCH!"

Proverbs 9:9 *Rebuke a wise man, and he will love you.*

To rebuke someone means to express sharp disproval or criticism of someone because of their behavior or actions. Some other words used to describe rebuke are: Reprove, Admonish, Reproach and to Chide. God has many ways of using people as a friendly reminder when our behaviors and actions are contrary to Him. A wise person receives a rebuke and does not become angry because they realize the person rebuking them is being used by God to help them change.

Have you ever been making a statement about something in a behavior or attitude not pleasing to God and someone responded to you in a manner that stopped you dead in your track? You knew you were wrong but how they responded felt like someone punched you in the stomach. Initially it did not feel good. You may have even gotten angry with that person. However, after you reflected on the matter you loved them even more than you did before they rebuked you.

Today as we look at this verse in Proverbs 9 I just want to share a few scriptures that I believe speak to the necessity of the rebuke, the results of the rebuke, and the reason for the rebuke.

Proverbs 27: 5 Open rebuke is better than love carefully concealed.

James 5:19,20 Brethren, if anyone wanders from the truth, and someone turns him back, let him know that he who turns a sinner from the error of his way will save a soul from death and cover a multitude of sins.

Proverbs 1:23 Turn at my rebuke; surely I will pour out my spirit on you; I will make my words known to you.

Luke 17:3,4 Take heed to yourselves. If your brother sins against you, rebuke him; and if he repents, forgive him. And if he sins against you seven times in a day, and seven times in a day returns to you, saying, "I repent", you shall forgive him.

II Timothy 4:2 (Amplified) Herald and preach the Word! Keep your sense of urgency [stand by, be at hand and ready], whether the opportunity seems to be favorable or unfavorable. [Whether it is convenient or inconvenient, whether it is welcome or unwelcome, you as the preacher of the Word are to show people in what way their lives are wrong.] and convince them, rebuking and correcting, warning and urging them, being unflagging and inexhaustible in patience and teaching.

REFLECTION:

1. Do you ever really think about how much your behavior directly impacts those around you?
2. Do you receive the rebuking of others well? Does it move you to change?
3. Are you bold/confident enough to rebuke others when the Lord is leading you to or do you fear how they will respond?
4. Has God been leading you to rebuke someone and as of right now you still haven't done it? Do it!
5. Has God used someone in your life to rebuke you and you are still angry with them? Go make amends today!

TEA:

As you explore today's Proverb why not take it all in while sipping on a cup of **Rose hips Tea**. Some of the great benefits of drinking **Rose hips Tea** are:

→ Rich in vitamin C
→ Has some cancer fighting properties
→ Helps reduce pain for people with osteoarthritis
→ Useful in lowering blood pressure
→ Has some cancer prevention benefits

enJOY!

YOU TALK TOO MUCH!

Verse 19 In the multitude of words sin is not lacking, But he who re-strains his lips is wise.

In the 1980's there was a song written by Run DMC that really sums up today's verse. As you read the lyrics to this song, think about why this verse reminds us that in the multitude of words sin is not lacking.

"You talk too much you never shut up; You talk too much you never shut up

Hey! You over there, I know about your kind You're like the independent network News on channel 9

Everywhere you go, no matter where you at, I said you talk about this and you talk about that

→ When the cat took your tongue, I say you took it right back

→ Your mouth is so big, one bite would kill a Big Mac

→ You talk too much you never shut up

→ I said you talk too much you never shut up

→ You talk about people, you don't even know

→ And you talk about places, you NEVER go

→ You talk about your girl, from head to toe

→ I said your mouth's moving fast, and your brain's moving slow

→ You talk too much you never shut up

→ I said you talk too much you never shut up............"

Of course the song is much longer, but I just wanted you to see a few verses.

Just to name a few things that are sin before God, too much talking that's not focused can lead to gossip, backbiting, complaining, mur-muring and lying. I would like to share some verses that supports today's verse in Proverbs 10.

Ephesians 4:29 Let no corrupt word proceed out of your mouth, but what is good for necessary edification, that it may impart grace to the hearers.

Proverbs 12:18 There is one who speaks like the piercings of a sword, But the tongue of the wise promotes health.

Matthew 12:36 But I say to you that for every idle word men may speak, they will give an account of it in the Day of Judgment.

Proverbs 18:21 Death and life are in the power of the tongue, And those who love it will eat its fruit.

Proverbs 17: 27,28 He who has knowledge spares his words, And a man of understanding is of a calm spirit. Even a fool is counted wise when he holds his peace; when he shuts his lips, he is considered perceptive.

Proverbs 26:22 The words of a talebearer are like tasty trifles, And they go down into the inmost body.

Proverbs 26: 28 A lying tongue hates those who are crushed by it, and a flattering mouth works ruin.

Psalm 141:3 Set a guard, O Lord, over my mouth; Keep watch over the doors of my lips.

Proverbs 21:23 Whoever guards his mouth and tongue Keeps his soul from trouble.

Proverbs 15:4 A wholesome tongue is a tree of life, But perverseness in it breaks the spirit.

Proverbs13:3 He who guards his mouth preserves his life, But he who opens wide his lips shall have destruction.

REFLECTION:

1. After reading the above verses, do you believe the Lord is requiring you to speak less and be mindful of what you say?
2. Write Proverbs 17:27,28 in your own words. How does it speak to you?
3. Before you speak you should always keep Matthew 12:36 at the forefront of your mind. Why?
4. Do you have any friends who hold you accountable for the things you say or do your friends encourage ungodly conversation?
5. If you are one who realizes you "talk too much", what are some things you can begin to do differently?

 TEA:

As you explore today's Proverb why not take it all in while sipping on a cup of **Ginger Tea**. Some of the great benefits of drinking **Ginger Tea** are:

→ Fights cancer
→ Protects against Alzheimer's disease
→ Helps with irritable bowel syndrome
→ Relieves gas
→ Relieves heartburn
→ Aids in weight loss
→ Suppresses appetite
→ Helps manage blood sugar levels
→ Helps with morning sickness
→ Reduces arthritic inflammation
→ Improves circulation
→ Stops motion sickness

enJOY!

ARE YOU A REVEALER OR A CONCEALER?

Verse 13 *A talebearer reveals secrets, But he who is of a faithful spirit conceals a matter.*

A talebearer is a person who maliciously gossips or reveals secrets. To Conceal means to keep secret; to prevent or avoid disclosing or divulging.

So the question today is, are you a revealer or a concealer? It's said that what comes out of our mouths is like toothpaste coming out of a tube of toothpaste. Once words comes out we can't get them back in.

Also, the Bible reminds us in Matthew 12:36 that for every idle word men speak, they will give an account in the Day of Judgment. So, one of the main reasons we should not reveal what others share is because God is very clear about the consequences of idle conversation.

Another reason should be out of loving the person who chooses to share. The Bible says that love covers... As Christians we should be trustworthy in everything. God has called us to be people who demonstrate integrity in all that we do and with every person we encounter. Let's journey through the word of God today and see what God has to say about it.

Talebearer:

Proverbs 16:28 A perverse person spreads strife, and a whisperer separates close friends. - Destroys friendships

Proverbs 20:19 A gossip reveals secrets; therefore do not associate with a babbler. - Cannot keep a secret

Psalm 101:5 One who secretly slanders a neighbor I will destroy.-Will be judged by God

Proverbs 18:8 The words of a whisperer are like delicious morsels; they go down into the inner body.

Gossip:

Proverbs 20:19 A gossip reveals secrets; therefore do not associate with a babbler

Psalm 141:3 set a guard over my mouth, O Lord; keep watch over the door of my lips

James 1:26 If any think they are religious, and do not bridle their tongues but deceive their hearts, their religion is worthless.

I Thessalonians 4:11 to aspire to live quietly, to mind your own affairs, and to work with your own hands......

Leviticus 19:16 You shall not go around as a slanderer among your people, and you shall not profit by the blood of your neighbor.

Faithful/Trustworthy:

Proverbs 20:6 Most men will proclaim each his own goodness, But who can find a faithful man?

Titus 2:7 in all things showing yourself to be a pattern of good works.....

Proverbs 10:9 He who walks with integrity walks securely, But he who perverts his ways will become known.

Proverbs 28:6 Better is the poor who walks in his integrity than one perverse in his ways, though he be rich.

Confidentiality:

Proverbs 25:9, 10 Debate your case with your neighbor, And do not disclose the secret to another; Lest he who hears it expose your shame, And your reputation be ruined.

Proverbs 17:9 He who covers a transgression seeks love, But he who repeats a matter seperates friends.

REFLECTION:

1. Are you trustworthy?
2. Are people comfortable sharing with you?
3. Have you ever been guilty of sharing something that was shared with you in confidence? Were you convicted afterwards? What did you learn from that?
4. When people think of you, do you think they think of you as a talebearer-one who repeats everything you hear or as a concealer-one who keeps everything confidential? Be honest with yourself and God.
5. If you are a talebearer go before the Lord, repent and ask Him to help you become more of a concealer.

TEA:

As you explore today's Proverb why not take it all in while sipping on a cup of **Cinnamon Tea**. Some of the greatest benefits of drinking **Cinnamon Tea** are:

→ It is an antioxidant
→ Lowers cholesterol
→ Fights viruses such as cold and flu viruses
→ It improves circulation
→ Reduces the pains and aches of arthritis
→ Lowers blood sugar levels
→ Helps with memory
→ Helps with weight loss

enJOY!

DON'T BE STUPID!

Verse 1 (KJV) Whoever loves instruction loves knowledge, But he who hates correction is stupid.

(Amplified) If you love learning, you love the discipline that goes with it- how shortsighted to refuse correction.

It never feels good to be corrected. However, our willingness to receive it helps us grow wiser. Pride is what gets in the way. Humility receives the correction and grows from it.

The Bible makes it very clear in Proverbs 11:2 When pride comes, then comes disgrace, but with humility comes wisdom.

Today let's take a look at loving correction (humility) vs. hating correction (pride).

Love correction (humility)	vs	Hate correction (Pride)
→ Proverbs 8:13		→ Colossians 3:12
→ Proverbs 11:2		→ Proverbs 16:5
→ Proverbs 18:12		→ Proverbs 21:24
→ Proverbs 22:4		→ Proverbs 29:23
→ Proverbs 15:33		→ Proverbs 26:12

REFLECTION:

1. Are you open to correction or do you get angry when you are corrected? Let's be honest!
2. When was the last time you received correction without becoming angry or arguing your point?
3. Could it be that you are too prideful to receive correction?
4. Are there only certain people that you are willing to receive correction from? Why?
5. Could you be missing God at work when you choose not to receive correction?

TEA:

As you explore today's Proverb why not take it all in while sipping on a cup of **Mint Tea**. Some of the great benefits of drinking **Mint Tea** are:

→ It is a fever reducer
→ It is good for digestive health
→ It reduces nausea or vomiting
→ It boost the immune system
→ It helps improve breath
→ It relieves mental stress
→ It relieves excess gas
→ It s good for coughs and colds

enJOY!

STOP IT!

Verses 10 By pride comes nothing but strife..........

In conflict a lot?

Always in an argument?

Check your pride meter. A heart of humility does not need to prove itself. A humble heart recognizes and embraces the idea that "God is my defense and my vindicator." A heart of humility also realizes that the Lord at times uses others to point things out in our lives.

Today let's take a look at what the Bible has to say about strife, pride and humility and let the Word of God dwell in you richly.

Pride	Strife	Humility
→ James 4:6	→ Proverbs 17:1	→ James 4:10
→ Proverbs 8:13	→ Proverbs 20:3	→ Philippians 2:3
→ Proverbs 11:12	→ Proverbs 17:14	→ Proverbs 11:2
→ Proverbs 16:18	→ Proverbs 17:19,20	→ Proverbs 16:19
→ Proverbs 21:24	→ Proverbs 18:6,7	→ Ephesians 4:2
→ Proverbs 29:23	→ 2 Timothy 2:22,23	→ Colossians 3:12
→ Psalm 10:4	→ Galatians 5:19-21	→ Proverbs 22:4
→ I Corinthians 13:4	→ James 4:1	→ I Peter 3:8
→ Proverbs 16:5	→ Proverbs 10:12	→ James 3:13

REFLECTION:

1. Today as you read be open and let God's Word speak to you.
2. The scriptures that speak to you the most, make them your memory scriptures for today.
3. As Christians, God has called us to a place of humility. Make it your aim to practice humility in your daily life. Denounce strife. Today journal about each time you practiced humility in your interactions.
4. Proverbs 20:3 It is honorable for a man to stop striving, Since any fool can start a quarrel. In your own words write out this verse. How can this help you the next time an opportunity comes up that could lead to an argument?
5. Proverbs 17:19 a. says He who loves transgression loves strife- What does it mean to love transgression?

TEA:

As you explore today's Proverb, why not take it all in while sipping on a cup of **Cranberry Tea**. Some of the greatest benefits of drinking **Cranberry Tea** are:

→ It can help burn fat.
→ Good for oral hygiene
→ Good for urinary tract health
→ Helps boosts immune system
→ Helps speed up metabolism
→ Helps reduce cholesterol levels in the body

enJOY!

SELF-CONSUMED!

Verse 14 The backslider in heart will be filled with his own ways, but a good man will be satisfied from above.

One word to describe "filled with his own ways" is – selfish. We live in a time where selfishness seems to be en-vogue. As you read verse 14 in Proverbs 14 it shows that a backslider in heart is a selfish person. In other words, to backslide means to relapse in bad habits or sinful behavior. Therefore, the individual who turns to old habits or returns to his sinful behaviors becomes self-seeking/selfish. His/her only desire is to please self and the flesh. They do not seek to please God. When you are consumed with yourself it's a good indication that you need to check your heart. It is a good chance you are backsliding.

Today let's look at a few scriptures that speak to Proverbs 14:14.

II Corinthians 5: 15 and He died for all, that those who live should live no longer for themselves, but for Him who died for them and rose again.

Romans 8:5 For those who live according to the flesh set their minds on the things of the flesh, but those who live in the Spirit, the things of the Spirit.

II Timothy 3:2 For men will be lovers of themselves, lovers of money, boasters, proud, blasphemers, disobedient to parents, unthankful, unholy........

Matthew 23:25 Woe to you, scribes and Pharisees, hypocrites! For you cleanse the outside of the cup and dish, but inside they are full of self-indulgence.

Galatians 5:19,20 Now the works of the flesh are evident, which are: adultery, fornication, uncleanness, lewdness, idolatry, sorcery, hatred, contentions, jealousies, outburst of wrath, selfish ambitions, dissensions, heresies.......

James 3:14-16 But if you have bitter envy and self-seeking in your hearts, do not boast and lie against the truth.

REFLECTION:

1. Are you a backslider in heart today? Check your pulse.
2. Which of these verses spoke directly to you?
3. What are some sinful behaviors/habits that you need to change?
4. Write a prayer using Philippians 2:2,3 as your guide that would help you to become less selfish.
5. Make a commitment to pray the prayer you created for the next 30 days.

 ## TEA:

As you explore today's Proverb why not take it all in while sipping on a cup of **Pomegranate Tea**. Some of the great benefits of drinking **Pomegranate Tea** are:

→ Rich in antioxidants
→ Good for the heart
→ Has anti-inflammatory properties
→ May reduce cholesterol levels
→ May lower blood pressure

enJOY!

BE ENCOURAGED! HE HEARS YOU!

Verse 8 ... *But the prayer of the upright is His delight.*

Verse 29 *The Lord is far from the wicked, But He hears the prayer of the righteous.*

There are times in our walk with Jesus that we really don't feel like He hears us. He may not answer a prayer we have been petitioning before Him for a long time. Sometimes He gives us an answer we don't want like NO. Sometimes He will require us to wait. Sometimes He just might answer YES right away. Other times it could be the sin in our lives that makes Him seem so far away from us. However, today's verses in Proverbs 15 encourages us to remain persistent in prayer because He hears the prayer of the upright. Luke 18:1 reminds us that we ought to pray and not to lose heart. Let's journey through some scriptures to see what God has to say.

Psalm 66:18 – 20 If I regard wickedness in my heart, The Lord will not hear; But certainly God has heard; He has given heed to the voice of my prayer. Blessed be God, Who has not turned away my prayer, nor His lovingkindness from me.

Psalm34:15 The eyes of the Lord are toward the righteous, And His ears are open to their cry.

Psalm 139:1-4 O Lord, Thou hast searched me and known me. You know my sitting down and my rising up; You understand my thought afar off. You comprehend my path and my lying down, And are acquainted with all of my ways. For there is not a word on my tongue, But behold, O Lord, You know it all together.

Hebrews 4:15,16 For we do not have a High Priest who cannot sympathize with our weaknesses, but was in all points tempted as we are, yet without sin. Let us therefore come boldly to the throne of grace, that we may obtain mercy and find grace in time of need.

John 16: 23,24 And in that day you will ask Me nothing. Most assuredly, I say to you, whatever you ask the Father in My name He will give. Until now you have asked nothing in my name. Ask, and you will receive, that your joy may be full.

Matthew 7:7,8 Ask and it will be given to you; seek and you will find; knock and it will be opened to you. For everyone who asks receives, and he who seeks finds, and to him who knocks it will be opened.

Matthew 6:6 But you, when you pray, go into your room, and when you have shut the door, pray to you Father who is in the secret place; and you Father who sees in secret will reward you openly.

John 14:13,14 And whatever you ask in My name, that I will do, that the Father may be glorifiedin the Son. If you ask anything in my name I will do it.

I Thessalonians 6:17 Pray without ceasing.

REFLECTIONS:

1. How is your prayer life? Could it be better?
2. Are you praying in faith?
3. Are you angry because your prayer has been delayed?
4. Do you trust that God knows what's best for you and He will answer your prayers accordingly?
5. Do you believe that God delights in answering your prayers?

TEA:

As you explore today's Proverb why not take it all in while sipping on a cup of **Nettle Tea**. Some of the benefits of drinking **Nettle Tea** are:

→ Boosts immunity
→ Relieves arthritis symptoms
→ Relieves menopausal symptoms
→ Helps with menstrual cramps and bloating
→ Reduces hypertension
→ Minimizes skin problems
→ Lessens nausea
→ Helps with IBS
→ May cure the common cold

enJOY!

ARE YOUR WORDS SWEET?

Verse 24 *Pleasant words are like honeycomb, sweetness to the soul and health to the bones.*

It was a myth when people used to say, "sticks and stones may break my bones but words will never hurt me." Words DO hurt. Some people in their lifetime can never get over something very hurtful that was said to them. Some have been so traumatized by words said to them they have become paralyzed and can't move past the hurt of what has been said.

Taking a look at today's verse in Proverbs 16, make a decision to use your tongue to speak pleasant words. Use your tongue to speak life into everyone you encounter. You are God's mouthpiece. How well are you representing Him with your mouth? Ephesians 4:29 reminds us to let No corrupt communication proceed out of our mouth, but what is good for necessary edification, that it may impart grace to the hearers. Let's take a close look at what God has to say.

Proverbs 18:21 Death and life are in the power of the tongue, and those who love it will eat its fruit.

Proverbs 12:18 There is one who speaks like the piercing of a sword, But the tongue of the wise promotes health.

Proverbs 15:4 A wholesome tongue is a tree of life, But perverseness in it breaks the spirit.

Proverbs 15:28 The heart of the righteous studies how to answer, But the mouth of the wicked pours forth evil.

Proverbs 15:23 A man has joy by the answer of his mouth, and a word spoken in due season, is good.

I Peter 3:10 For He who would love life And see good days, Let him refrain his tongue from evil, and his lips from speaking deceit.

II Samuel 23:2 The Spirit of the lord spoke by me, And His word was on my tongue.

REFLECTIONS:

1. What kind of words are you speaking?
2. Are your words full of life to those you speak with? Are your words words of death to those you speak with?
3. What does it mean when it's said that some words hurt and some words heal? / How can you do better at making sure that all of your words are pleasant?
4. Today write in your journal every conversation you have. Were you intentional about making your words pleasant?
5. Your words may be the only pleasant words some people receive. Make it your business to speak pleasant words into every life you encounter.

TEA:

As you explore today's Proverb why not take it all in while sipping on a cup of **Lavender Tea**. Some of the great benefits of drinking **Lavender Tea** are:

→ Relieves indigestion
→ Insomnia relief
→ May treat migraines
→ Helps sooth gas , colic and an upset stomach
→ Can help reduce cough, bronchitis and other respiratory issues

enJOY!

WHAT ARE YOU WILLING TO LISTEN TO?

Verse 4 *An evildoer gives head to false lips: A liar listens eagerly to a spiteful tongue.*

The Message-(Evil people relish malicious conversation; The ears of liars itch for dirty gossip.)

Questions: What kind of conversation are you willing to listen to? What conversations do you engage in when you know that you should not? How do you stop these types of conversations before they get started?

In this verse the Bible says if you are willing to listen to inappropriate conversation you are an evil doer and a liar. Today let's take a look at what God has to say about evil doers and liars in His Word.

Liar:

Proverbs 12:22 Lying lips are an abomination to the Lord, But those who deal truthfully are His delight.

Psalm 63:11 But the king shall rejoice in God; Everyone who swears by Him shall glory; But the mouth of those who speak lies shall be stopped.

Exodus 23:1 You shall not circulate a false report. Do not put your hand with the wicked to be an unrighteous witness.

Proverbs 19:9 a false witness will not go unpunished, and he who breathes out lies will perish.

Proverbs 14:5 A faithful witness does not lie, but a false witness breathes out lies.

John 8:44 You are of your father the devil, and to do your father's desires. He was a murderer from the beginning, and has nothing to do with truth, because there is no truth in him. When he lies, he speaks out of his own character, for he is a liar and the father of lies.

Evildoer:

Psalm 26:5 I have hated the assembly of evildoers, And will not sit with the wicked.

Psalm 34:16 The face of the Lord is against those who do evil, To cut off the remembrance of them from the earth.

Psalm 101:8 Early I will destroy all the wicked of the land, That I may cut off all the evildoers from the city of the Lord.

Job 8:20 Behold, God will not cast away the blameless, Nor will He uphold evildoers.

James 4:17 Therefore, whoever knows the right thing to do and fails to do it, for him it is sin.

Be careful what you listen to, according to the above verse you will be considered an evil doer and a liar if you listen to false lips and a spiteful tongue.

REFLECTION:

1. Today do something different for your quiet time. Take a long walk and listen intently to God. Ponder Proverb 17:4.
2. Does it speak specifically to you in any way?
3. Is there some commandment to follow?
4. Is there something you need to change?
5. How can you be a change agent in someone else's life? (If you stop someone before they start a conversation you might challenge their behavior)
6. How was the entire experience walking and talking with God?
7. Make a decision to let the Lord uses you to stop unfruitful conversations.

TEA:

As you explore today's Proverb why not take it all in while sipping on a cup of **Lemon Balm Tea**. Some of the great benefits of drinking **Lemon Balm Tea** are:

→ Calms the mind.
→ Encourages restful sleep.
→ Sharpens memory and Problem solving skills.
→ It's an antioxidant
→ Protects brain cells
→ Supports the liver

enJOY!

SINFUL SELFISHNESS

Verse 1 A man who isolates himself seeks his own desire; he rages against sound judgment.

The Message version. Loners who care only for themselves spit on the common good.

Show me a loner and I tell you he/she cares only about themselves. Selfishness is rooted in pride. Pride is the exact opposite of humility and therefore a sin before God. God resists the proud but gives grace to the humble.

Philippians 2 can be used as a blueprint to help become less selfish. Today I ask you to read it. As you reflect on it let the principles of Jesus guide you.

Verse 2 (1) fulfill ye My joy

1. By being like minded
2. Having the same love
3. Being of one accord, of one mind

Verse 3 (2) let nothing be done through selfish ambition or conceit but in lowliness of mind

Verse 3 (3) Let each esteem others better than himself

Verse 4 (4) Let each of you look out not only for his own interests, but also for the interests of others.

Verse 5 (5) Let this mind be in you which is also in Christ Jesus.....

Verse 7 (6) 1. Made Himself of no reputation 2. Took on the form of a servant

Verse 8 (7) 3. He humbled Himself 4. Became obedient to the point of death on the cross.

REFLECTION:

It is one thing to have alone time. It is quite another thing to spend most of your time in isolation. According to our verse today, if the ladder is true then selfishness plays a role in the believer's life.

1. Today, take time to think about it. Ask yourself is my alone time healthy and necessary or do I spend the majority of my time in unhealthy isolation?
2. Ask the Lord to help you to discern which of the above is true.
3. Ask the Lord to surround you with a healthy group of like-minded friends if you find yourself spending most of your time in isolation.
4. Look for opportunities to serve others.
5. This week memorize Philippians 2: 2-8. Yes you can do it!

 TEA:

As you explore today's Proverb take it all in while sipping on a cup of **Cardamom Tea**. Some of the great benefits of drinking **Cardamom Tea** are:

→ Reduces risk of hypertension.
→ Relieves headaches.
→ Strengthens weak hair.
→ Treats scalp irritation and itchiness.
→ Heals digestive illnesses
→ Provides immunity.

enJOY!

ONE ACT OF KINDNESS DAILY!

Verse 22 What is desired in a man is kindness...

"You cannot do a kindness too soon, for you never know how soon it will be too late."- Ralph Waldo Emerson

"Kindness is the language which the deaf can hear and the blind can see."- Mark Twain

"Love and kindness are never waisted. They bless the one who receives them, and they bless you, the giver."- Barbara de Angelos

"Wherever there is a human being there is an opportunity for kindness."- Licius Annaeus Seneca

As we look at today's verse let's explore what the Bible has to say about kindness.

Look up each verse below. What do they say about kindness?

Ephesians 4:32_____

Hebrews 6:10_____

Galatians 5:22_____

Luke 6:35_____

Colossians 3:12 _____

Proverbs 3:3_____

Micah 6:8_____

Hebrews 13:2_____

Romans 12:10_____

REFLECTIONS:

1. Can you honestly say that you make it your goal to show kindness to everyone you encounter?
2. What are some things you can do to become consistent at being kind?
3. Are you able to demonstrate kindness to those who are unkind?
4. At home, on your job, in your day to day activities who are some people who could benefit from your kindness?
5. Every day this week make it your aim to demonstrate at least one act of kindness. Then try it for a month. Let kindness become who you are.

TEA:

As you explore today's Proverb take it all in while sipping on a cup of **Milk Thistle Tea**. Some of the great benefits of drinking **Milk Thistle Tea** are:

→ Sometimes used as a natural treatment for liver problems.
→ Can help lower cholesterol.
→ Helps lower blood sugar. For people with type 2 diabetes.
→ It is an antioxidant
→ It can help lower cholesterol.

enJOY!

O TO BE FAITHFUL!

Verse 6 Most men will proclaim each his own goodness, But who can find a faithful man?

Faithfulness is defined as the quality of being loyal and reliable. As we ponder today's verse let's look at examples in the Bible that demonstrate faithfulness to man as well as how we are called to be faithful to God.

Faithfulness to Man

→ Ruth and Naomi – Read Ruth 1:1-17
→ Elizabeth and Mary – Read Luke 1:1-56
→ David and Jonathan – Read I Samuel 18:1-4
→ Esther and Mordacai – Read Esther 4:1-17
→ Gomer and Hosea – Read the entire book of Hosea.... AMAZING!

Faithfulness to God

Psalm 31:23 – Oh, love the Lord, all you His saints! For the lord preserves the faithful, and fully repays the proud person.

I Kings 2:3,4 – And keep the charge of the Lord your God: to walk in His ways, to keep His statutes, His commandments, His judgments, and His testimonies, as it is written in the law of Moses, that you may prosper in all that you do wherever you turn; that the Lord may fulfill His word which He spoke concerning me, saying, If your sons take heed to their way, to walk before me in truth with all their heart and with all their soul, " He said, you shall not lack a man on the throne of Israel."

Deuteronomy 29:9 Therefore keep the words of this covenant, and do them, that you may prosper in all that you do.

I Samuel 12:24 Only fear the Lord, and serve Him in truth with all your heart; for consider what great things He has done for you.

I Timothy 1:12 And I thank Christ Jesus our Lord who has enabled me, because He counted me faithful, putting me into the ministry, although I was formerly a blasphemer, a persecutor, and an insolent man; but I obtained mercy because I did it ignorantly in unbelief.

Matthew 25:21 His lord said to him, Well done, good and faithful servant; you were faithful over a few things, I will make you ruler over many things. Enter into the joy of your lord.

Today's readings gave very clear pictures of what it looks like to faithful to man and why we should be faithful to God.

One final thought:

Proverbs 28:20 – A faithful man will abound with blessings...

REFLECTIONS:

1. Are you faithful?
2. Would your family, friends, co-workers, employer, church family etc. consider you faithful?
3. Are you faithful in doing the things the Lord has asked you to do?
4. Are you faithful in spending time with the Lord? How is your prayer life? Are you consistently reading His word?
5. Write down some things that you desire to be more faithful at and invite a friend to pray for you and hold you accountable.

This week read the entire book of Hosea to see a great picture of faithfulness. You will see the faithfulness of Hosea. I promise it will bless you! Journal what you learn from this reading.

TEA:

As you explore today's Proverb take it all in while sipping on a cup of **Echinacea Tea**. Some of the great benefits of **Echinacea Tea** are:

→ It can be used to fight infections.
→ It can reduce cold symptoms.
→ Fights chronic fatigue.
→ Helps with migraines.
→ Fights against gum disease.
→ Helps with urinary tract and yeast infections.

enJOY!

WHERE WOULD HE PREFER TO LIVE?

Verse 9 Better to dwell in a corner of a housetop, than in a house shared with a contentious woman.

Verse 19 Better to dwell in the wilderness, than with a contentious and angry woman.

The message version: Verse 9 Better to live in a tumble down shack than to share a mansion with a nagging spouse.

Verse 19 Better to live in a tent in the wild than with a cross and petulant (sulky or bad tempered) spouse.

Today as we explore this verse my dear sisters I ask you to close your eyes and envision the corner of a housetop and the wilderness. Got it?! If you are a contentious woman your husband would prefer to live in those places and not in the home with you. You ever wonder why he does not like being home? Or wonder why he shuts down when he gets home? Consider the atmosphere you create for him. Just as God shows up where there is praise so it is with a man. He is willfully present where there is praise and not contention.

Consider the following verses:

→ Proverbs 9:13 A foolish woman is clamorous; She is simple, and knows nothing.

→ Proverbs 10:14 Wise people store up knowledge, But the mouth of the foolish is near destruction.

→ Proverbs 13:3 He who guards his mouth preserves his life, But he who opens wide his lips shall have destruction.

→ Proverbs 14:1 The wise woman builds her house, But the foolish pulls down with her hands.

→ Proverbs 14:3 In the mouth of a fool is a rod of pride, But the lips of the wise will preserve them.

→ Proverbs 15:1 A soft answer turns away wrath, But harsh words stir up anger.

→ Proverbs 16:23 The heart of the wise teaches his mouth, And adds learning to his lips.

→ Proverbs 18: 6, 7 A fool's lips enter into contention, And his mouth calls for blows. A fool's mouth is his destruction, And his lips are the snare of his soul.

My dear sisters I encourage you to change the temperature in your home and as a result bless your marriage.

Make your home a place that he wants to be.

REFLECTIONS:

1. Ladies consider 31 days of praise for your husband and watch it change the atmosphere of your home.
2. Journal your journey each day.
3. Solicit a friend to do it along with you and pray for you as you change the atmosphere of your home.
4. Before you speak always keep in mind Proverbs 31:12 She does him good and not evil all the days of her life. Proverbs 31:26 She opens her mouth with wisdom and on her tongue is the law of kindness.
5. If he were asked, where would he say he would prefer to live?

TEA:

As you explore today's Proverb, take it all in while sipping on a cup of **Blackberry Tea**. Some of the great benefits of **Blackberry Sage Tea** are:

→ Helps with digestive health.
→ Helps keep bones strong and healthy.
→ Aids in enhancing memory.
→ Helps with weight management.
→ Improves vision.
→ Helps keep the heart healthy.

enJOY!

ARE YOU WILLING TO GIVE FREELY?

Verse 9 He who has a generous eye will be blessed, For he gives his bread to the poor.

Giving is what we are called to do as Christians. Understanding stewardship is recognizing that nothing that we have is our own. Everything we have belongs to God. Knowing this should make it easy to give. Yet we live in a society of takers and not givers. It is God who gives us the ability to produce wealth. (Deuteronomy 8:18) His intentions are that we become conduits of His resources to bless those who are in need or less fortunate. Today as we focus on Proverbs 22:9 Let us look closely at what else God has to say through His Word about giving.

Proverbs 19:17 He who has pity on the poor lends to the Lord. And He will pay back what he has given.

Proverbs 28:27 He who gives to the poor will not lack, But he who hides his eyes will have many curses.

Luke 3 :10,11 He answered and said to them, " He who has two tunics, let him give to him who has none; and he who has food, let him do likewise."

Matthew 25: 35-40 for I was hungry and you gave Me food; I was thirsty and you gave Me drink; I was a stranger and you to Me in; I was naked and you clothed Me; I was sick and you visited Me; I was in prison and you came to Me. Then the righteous will answer Him, saying, Lord when did we see You hungry and feed You, or thirsty and give You drink? When did we see You a stranger and take You in, or naked clothe You? Or when did we see You sick or in prison, and come to You? And the King will answer to them, Assuredly, I say to you, inasmuch as you did it to one of the least of these My brethren, you did it to Me.

Acts 2:44,45 Now all who believed were together, and had all things in common, and sold their possessions and goods, and divided them among all, as anyone has need.

James 2:14-17 What does it profit, my brethren, if someone says he has faith but does not have works? Can faith save him? If a brother or sister is naked or destitute of daily food, and one of you say to them, Depart in peace, be warmed and filled, but you do not give them the things which are needed for the body, what does it profit? Thus also faith by itself, if it does not have works is dead.

I John 3:17 But whoever has this world's goods and sees his brother in need, and shuts up his heart from him, how does the love of God abide in him?

Philippians 2:4 Let each of you look out not only for his own interests, but also for the interests of others.

Deuteronomy 15: 11 For the poor will never cease from the land; therefore I command you, saying, You shall open your hand wide to your brother, to your poor and your needy, in your land.

REFLECTIONS:

1. Through the passages of scriptures given to you today how has God spoken to you about giving to the poor?
2. Do you look for opportunities to give to the poor?
3. Begin to look for more and more opportunities to let God use you as a vessel of His love to give to the poor.
4. Ezekiel 18:7-9 and Ezekiel 18:16-18 speaks of giving and not giving. Take time today to rewrite the verses so that they become personal to you.
5. Make it a priority this week to look for opportunities to give.

TEA:

As you explore today's Proverb, take it all in while sipping on a cup of **Hawthorn Tea**. Some of the great benefits of drinking **Hawthorn Tea** are:

→ Good for cardiovascular health
→ Good for reducing anxiety
→ Reduces high blood pressure
→ Good for diarrhea and stomach pain
→ Reduces high cholesterol

enJOY!

ENVY IS A STRONG WORD!

Verse 17 Do not let your heart envy sinners, But be zealous for the fear of the Lord all day.

I hear you already. Seems like sinners are prospering all around us, true, but what profits a man if he gains the world and loses his soul? Yes, they seem to enjoy the finer things in life and yes, it may seem like life is not fair but the end of life without Jesus is weeping and gnashing of teeth and the end of a Christian's life on earth is a place in heaven. We live in a world of immediate gratification so it may seem like sinners have it going on, but God!

Today let's look at what the Bible has to say about why we should not envy sinners.

Psalm 37

The Heritage of the Righteous and the Calamity of the Wicked

Do not fret because of evildoers,
Nor be envious of the workers of iniquity.
²For they shall soon be cut down like the grass,
And wither as the green herb.

³ Trust in the LORD, and do good;
Dwell in the land, and feed on His faithfulness.
⁴ Delight yourself also in the LORD,
And He shall give you the desires of your heart.

⁵ Commit your way to the LORD,
Trust also in Him,
And He shall bring it to pass.
⁶ He shall bring forth your righteousness as the light,
And your justice as the noonday.

⁷ Rest in the LORD, and wait patiently for Him;
Do not fret because of him who prospers in his way,
Because of the man who brings wicked schemes to pass.

⁸ Cease from anger, and forsake wrath;
Do not fret—it only causes harm.

⁹ For evildoers shall be cut off;
But those who wait on the LORD,
They shall inherit the earth.
¹⁰ For yet a little while and the wicked shall be no more;
Indeed, you will look carefully for his place,
But it shall be no more.
¹¹ But the meek shall inherit the earth,
And shall delight themselves in the abundance of peace.

¹² The wicked plots against the just,
And gnashes at him with his teeth.
¹³ The Lord laughs at him,
For He sees that his day is coming.
¹⁴ The wicked have drawn the sword
And have bent their bow,
To cast down the poor and needy,
To slay those who are of upright conduct.
¹⁵ Their sword shall enter their own heart,
And their bows shall be broken.

¹⁶ A little that a righteous man has
Is better than the riches of many wicked.
¹⁷ For the arms of the wicked shall be broken,
But the LORD upholds the righteous.

¹⁸ The LORD knows the days of the upright,
And their inheritance shall be forever.
¹⁹ They shall not be ashamed in the evil time,
And in the days of famine they shall be satisfied.
²⁰ But the wicked shall perish;
And the enemies of the LORD,
Like the splendor of the meadows, shall vanish.
Into smoke they shall vanish away.

²¹ The wicked borrows and does not repay,
But the righteous shows mercy and gives.
²² For those blessed by Him shall inherit the earth,
But those cursed by Him shall be cut off.

²³ The steps of a good man are ordered by the LORD,
And He delights in his way.
²⁴ Though he fall, he shall not be utterly cast down;
For the LORD upholds him with His hand.

²⁵ I have been young, and now am old;
Yet I have not seen the righteous forsaken,
Nor his descendants begging bread.
²⁶ He is ever merciful, and lends;
And his descendants are blessed.

²⁷ Depart from evil, and do good;
And dwell forevermore.
²⁸ For the LORD loves justice,
And does not forsake His saints;
They are preserved forever,
But the descendants of the wicked shall be cut off.
²⁹ The righteous shall inherit the land,
And dwell in it forever.

³⁰ The mouth of the righteous speaks wisdom,
And his tongue talks of justice.
³¹ The law of his God is in his heart;
None of his steps shall slide.

³² The wicked watches the righteous,
And seeks to slay him.
³³ The LORD will not leave him in his hand,
Nor condemn him when he is judged.

³⁴ Wait on the LORD,
And keep His way,
And He shall exalt you to inherit the land;
When the wicked are cut off, you shall see it.
³⁵ I have seen the wicked in great power,
And spreading himself like a native green tree.
³⁶ Yet he passed away,[a] and behold, he was no more;
Indeed I sought him, but he could not be found.

37 Mark the blameless man, and observe the upright;
For the future of that man is peace.
38 But the transgressors shall be destroyed together;
The future of the wicked shall be cut off.

39 But the salvation of the righteous is from the LORD;
He is their strength in the time of trouble.
40 And the LORD shall help them and deliver them;
He shall deliver them from the wicked,
And save them,
Because they trust in Him.

Psalm 73

The tragedy of the wicked, and the Blessedness of Trust in God.

Truly God is good to Israel,
To such as are pure in heart.
2 But as for me, my feet had almost stumbled;
My steps had nearly slipped.
3 For I was envious of the boastful,
When I saw the prosperity of the wicked.
4 For there are no pangs in their death,
But their strength is firm.
5 They are not in trouble as other men,
Nor are they plagued like other men.
6 Therefore pride serves as their necklace;
Violence covers them like a garment.
7 Their eyes bulge[a] with abundance;
They have more than heart could wish.
8 They scoff and speak wickedly concerning oppression;
They speak loftily.
9 They set their mouth against the heavens,
And their tongue walks through the earth.
10 Therefore his people return here,
And waters of a full cup are drained by them.
11 And they say, "How does God know?
And is there knowledge in the Most High?"
12 Behold, these are the ungodly,

Who are always at ease;
They increase in riches.
¹³ Surely I have cleansed my heart in vain,
And washed my hands in innocence.
¹⁴ For all day long I have been plagued,
And chastened every morning.
¹⁵ If I had said, "I will speak thus,"
Behold, I would have been untrue to the generation of Your children.
¹⁶ When I thought how to understand this,
It was too painful for me—
¹⁷ Until I went into the sanctuary of God;
Then I understood their end.
¹⁸ Surely You set them in slippery places;
You cast them down to destruction.
¹⁹ Oh, how they are brought to desolation, as in a moment!
They are utterly consumed with terrors.
²⁰ As a dream when one awakes,
So, Lord, when You awake,
You shall despise their image.
²¹ Thus my heart was grieved,
And I was vexed in my mind.
²² I was so foolish and ignorant;
I was like a beast before You.
²³ Nevertheless I am continually with You;
You hold me by my right hand.
²⁴ You will guide me with Your counsel,
And afterward receive me to glory.
²⁵ Whom have I in heaven but You?
And there is none upon earth that I desire besides You.
²⁶ My flesh and my heart fail;
But God is the strength of my heart and my portion forever.
²⁷ For indeed, those who are far from You shall perish;
You have destroyed all those who desert You for harlotry.
²⁸ But it is good for me to draw near to God;
I have put my trust in the Lord GOD,
That I may declare all Your works.

REFLECTION:

1. Do you envy the wicked? Be honest!
2. Why do you envy the wicked?
3. What are the benefits of trusting God?
4. Do you find comfort in knowing the benefits of trusting God?
5. How did Psalm 37 speak to you? Does it change your perspective?
6. How did Psalm 73 speak to you? Does it change your perspective?

TEA:

As you explore today's Proverb, take it all in while sipping on a cup of **Yerba - Mate Tea**. Some of the great benefits of drinking **Yerba - Mate Tea** are:

→ Rich in antioxidants
→ Enhances your ability to focus
→ Enhances physical endurance
→ Aids digestion
→ Helps control your weight
→ Supports cardiovascular health

enJOY!

GET UP AND KEEP GOING!

Verse 16a. For a righteous man may fall seven times, And rise again...

Grace - undeserving favor of God.

As Christians we are blessed to be saved by grace through faith. Thank God! It is great to know that we serve a God who is forever extending His grace towards us. Where would we be if not for His grace? Not only does He extend His grace, but He also extends forgiveness of sin. (Psalm 103, Psalm 66, I John 1:9)

Today's verse make me think of the following verses:

Romans 7:14 -25 For we know that the law is spiritual, but I am carnal, sold under sin. For what I am doing, I do not understand. For what I will to do, that I do not practice; but what I hate that I do. If, then, I do what I will not to do, I agree with the law that it is good. But now, it is no longer I who do it, but the sin that dwells in me. For I know that in me (that is, in my flesh) nothing good dwells; for to will is present with me , but how to perform what is good I do not find. For the good that I will to do, I do not do, but the evil I will not to do, that I practice. Now if I do what I will not to do, it is no longer I who do it, but sin that dwells in me. I find then a law, that evil is present with me, the one who wills to do good. For I delight in the law of God according to the inward man. But I see another law in my members, warring against the law of my mind, and bringing me into captivity to the law of sin which is in my members. O wretched man that I am! Who will deliver me from this body of death? I thank God through Jesus Christ our Lord! So the, with the mind I myself serve the law of God, but with the flesh the law of sin.

Romans 8: 1 There is therefore now no condemnation to those who are in Christ Jesus, who do not walk according to the flesh, but according to the Spirit.

II Corinthians 12: 5-10 Of such a one I will boast; yet of myself I will not boast, except in my infirmities. For though I might desire to boast, I will not be a fool; for I will speak the truth. But I will refrain lest anyone should think of me above what he sees me to be or hears from me. And lest I should be exalted above measure by the abundance of the revelations, a thorn in the flesh was given to me, a messenger of Satan to buffet me, lest I be exalted above measure.

Concerning this thing I pleaded with the Lord three times that it might depart from me . And He said to me, "My grace is sufficient for you, for My strength is made perfect in weakness." Therefore, most gladly I will rather boast in my infirmities, that the power of Christ may rest upon me. Therefore, I take pleasure in infirmities, in reproaches, in needs, in persecutions, in distresses, for Christ's sake. For when I am weak, then I am strong.

Grace means we are receiving something we don't deserve. But God!

Forgiveness means to wipe the slate clean, to pardon, to cancel a debt. Because of God's grace and his forgiveness, when we do fall He is quick to show us that He is a God of another chance.

REFLECTION:

1. Take time to really study Romans 7:14- Romans 8:1. In your journal write out the way you see God's grace and his forgiveness embedded in those verses.
2. Read 2 Corinthians 12:5-10 again. How does each verses speak about grace? How do they speak to you specifically?
3. Are you harder on yourself than God is? Why do you think that you are?
4. When you fall, do you immediately confess and receive God's forgiveness or does it take you a while to get back up and get going?
5. How has today's verse personally spoken to you?

TEA:

As you explore today's Proverb why not take it all in while sipping on a cup of **Acai Tea**. Some of the great benefits of drinking **Acai Tea** are:

→ Boosts energy levels
→ Promotes healthier vision
→ Improves mental sharpness
→ Reduces inflammation
→ Rich in antioxidants
→ Regulates blood sugar
→ Keeps the heart healthy
→ Strengthens immunity

enJOY!

LOVE YOUR ENEMIES

Verses 21,22 (Message) *If you see your enemy hungry, go buy him lunch; if he's thirsty, bring him a drink. Your generosity will surprise him with goodness, and God will look after you.*

This morning just as I was preparing to type this, I was prompted by the Holy Spirit to reach out to someone who naturally I would like to do the extreme opposite. In this current season the Lord has me in, living life in total obedience the first time, I obeyed. In our humanity I would say it is almost impossible to do what today's verse encourages us to do but with God all things are possible. When we obey God we reap the benefits of obedience and in this case the person or people we are instructed to be a blessing to truly get to experience the love of God through us.

In order to love our enemies we must first have a love for God. (John 14:15) Out of total obedience to God we are, through Christ (Philippians4:13), able to love our enemies.

Today we are going to take a look at a few scriptures. As we look at the scriptures really take time to reflect on what God has to say about our enemies. Ultimately, in everything that we do we should glorify God.

Proverbs 16:7 When a man's ways please the Lord, He makes even his enemies to be at peace with him.

Matthew 5:33,34 You have heard that it was said, "You shall love your neighbor and hate your enemy", But I say to you, love your enemies, bless those who curse you, do good to those who hate you, and pray for those who spitefully use you and persecute you, that you may be sons of your Father in heaven; for He makes the sunrise on the evil and on the good, and sends down rain on the just and the unjust.

Luke 6:27-36 But I say to you who hear: Love your enemies, do good to those who hate you, bless those who curse you, and pray for those who spitefully use you. To him who strikes you on one cheek, offer the other also. And from him who takes away your cloak, do not withhold your tunic either. Give to everyone who asks of you. And from him who takes away your goods do not ask them back. And just as you want men to do to you, you also do likewise. But if you love those who love you, what credit is that to you? For even sinners do the same. And if you lend to those from whom you hope to receive back, what credit is that to you? For even sinners lend to sinners and receive much back. But love your enemies, do good, and lend, hoping for nothing in return; and your reward will be great, and you, will be sons of the Most High. Foe He is kind to the unthankful and evil.

Romans 12:20 Therefore, "If your enemy is hungry, feed him; If he is thirsty, give him drink. For in doing so you will heap coals of fire on his head."

Psalm 23:5 You prepare a table before me in the presence of my enemies...

REFLECTION:

1. Take time today to strategically develop a plan of how you will become a blessing to someone that you would consider your enemy. Journal it.
2. Journal how it made you feel and make it a point to address those feelings.
3. What was the response of your enemy?
4. Make a commitment to pray consistently for your enemy.
5. Be reminded that what we do as Christians should fully please the Lord.(Colossians 3:17)

TEA:

As you experience today's Proverb, take it all in while sipping on a cup of **Blueberry Tea**. Some of the great benefits of **Blueberry Tea** are:

→ Supply Antioxidants
→ Reduces risks if diabetes
→ Boosts immunity
→ Prevents dehydration
→ A good source of vitamin C
→ Helps with digestive health

enJOY!

DON'T DO IT!

Verse 11 *As a dog returns to his own vomit, so a fool repeats his folly.*

Nike symbol says Just Do It! In today's devotion I am pleading with you ....Don't Do It!

Do you constantly see yourself on a merry go round repeating things that you know you should not be? You know they say the definition of insanity is doing the same things expecting different results.

I have a dog and I have witnessed him vomiting and then returning to it to sniff it and sometimes lick at it. Sounds disgusting right? That's how disgusting we are when we continue in the same cycles of behaviors. God gives us ways of escape I Corinthians 10:13. Yet we continue in sinful patterns of behaviors not pleasing to Him. So how do we stop the disgusting cycle? I am glad you asked.

The change begins with having proper thought patterns. Our minds must be renewed (Ephesians 4:22-24). Our minds must be changed (Romans 12:2) (2 Corinthians 10:4,5). Our minds must be continuously occupied (Psalm 119:11, Psalm 119:15,16, Psalm 110:48, Psalm 119:81, Psalm 119:97, Psalm 119:105).

I wish I could tell you that there was some quick fix. Such is not the case. Our only victory over returning to folly is by consistently asking for the Lord to help us as we pray daily and daily meditating on His word and allowing His word to dwell in us richly.

We must be sure to ask God to direct our every move so that we are aligned with His word.

REFLECTIONS:

1. Take time today to read every scripture given in today's devotion. Ask God to allow His word to dwell in you richly. (Colossians 3:16)

2. Ask the Lord to daily direct your steps. (Psalm 119:133)

3. Meditate on His word daily. (Psalm 1:1-6)

4. What are some things that you find yourself continuously returning to? Ask the Lord to make them as disgusting as it is for a dog to return to his vomit.

5. Are you sick and tired of being sick and tired? Take at least one of the things you shared in question 4 and share with someone allowing them to hold you accountable.

TEA:

As you explore today's Proverb, take it all in while sipping on a cup of **Raspberry Tea**. Some of the great benefits of drinking **Raspberry Tea** are:

→ Great anti-inflammatory properties
→ Great antioxidant Properties
→ Can protect against cancer
→ Has heart benefits
→ Some women use it for painful periods
→ Some women use it for morning sickness

enJOY!

WHO ARE YOU SHARPENING?

Verse 17 As iron sharpens iron, so a man sharpens the countenance of a friend.

When I think of sharpening, my mind immediately goes to the story of Mary and Elizabeth in Luke 1. Mary is told, by an angel, that she is pregnant. I am sure at that point she experienced a gamut of emotions concerning this news. Shortly after that news, she was also informed that her cousin Elizabeth was with child. She immediately goes to support Elizabeth. As I read this story in Luke I see so many awesome character traits in Mary that demonstrates what it means to sharpen the countenance of a friend. According to the Oxford Dictionary to sharpen means to improve or cause to improve. Some of the characteristics of sharpening a friends' countenance in Luke 1 are:

→ Prayerfully listening to God – Luke 1 :35,36
→ A love for God- Luke 1:46-55
→ A selfless love for others – Luke 1:39-45,56
→ A commitment of time during a crucial season – Luke 1:56
→ Encouragement through the birthing process of new seasons – Luke 1:56

Below are some other scriptures that focus on friendship:

→ Job 2:11
→ Luke 6:31
→ Proverbs 18:24
→ Proverbs 19:20
→ Proverbs 24:5
→ Proverbs 13:20
→ Proverbs 27:5,6
→ Ecclesiastes 4:9,10
→ Proverbs17:17
→ Proverbs 12:26
→ Proverbs 27:9

REFLECTION:

1. What does "iron sharpening iron" mean to you?
2. Who are you sharpening?
3. Whose life is more blessed because of your presence in it?
4. What relationships are you being sharpened by?
5. Are you selfless enough to journey through a season with someone as Mary was with Elizabeth?
6. Which place to you find yourself in the most, sharpening or desiring to be sharpened? Why?

TEA:

As you explore today's Proverb why not take it all in while sipping on a cup of **Black Tea**. Some of the great benefits of drinking **Black Tea** are:

→ Improves Oral health
→ Antioxidants
→ A better heart
→ Healthy bones
→ Lowers the risk of diabetes
→ Better Immune system
→ Healthy digestive tract

As you explore today's Proverb why not take it all in while sipping on a cup of Black Tea.

enJOY!

TALK ABOUT IT!

Verse 13 He who covers sins will not prosper, But whoever confess and forsake them will have mercy.

As a former instructor of a twelve steps with God class one of the books we used, Raphas 12 Step Program by Robert S. McGee, did an excellent job at laying out this scripture by laying out what's called the CROP process.

Confession. Repentance. Obedience. Praise.

- → Confession – True confession is agreeing with God about sin. I John 1:9
- → Repentance – turning away from sin to God. 2 Chronicles 7:14
- → Obedience – doing what God says no matter what. I Samuel 15:22
- → Praise – scripture tells us to give thanks and praise to God in everything. I Thessalonians 5:18

Being consistent with confessing our sins, repenting of our sins, walking in obedience to God no matter what will certainly result in giving God praise.

Making the CROP process a part of our daily life can definitely result in joy for our journey.

REFLECTIONS:

1. Do you consider yourself to be a person who is transparent with God?
2. Do you believe God appreciates you being transparent?
3. What are some things that you think you are hiding from Him even right now?
4. Are you hindering your own prayers from being answered because of unconfessed sin in your life?
5. Today have a transparent talk with God confessing your sins, repenting of your sins, deciding to walk in obedience to God and then begin to praise God for the victories.

TEA:

As you explore today's Proverb, why not take it all in while sipping on a cup of **Rooibos Tea**. Some of the great benefits of drinking **Rooibos Tea** are:

→ Rich in antioxidants
→ Relieves hypertension
→ Helps with preventing diabetic complications.
→ Boosts the digestive tract
→ Improves blood circulation
→ Promotes healthy hair

enJOY!

SELF – CONTROL?!

Verse 11 *A fool vents all his feelings, But a wise man holds them back.*

As Christians we are expected to exercise self- control in every area of our life. (Galatians 5:22,23) James reminds us of how difficult it can be to tame the tongue. (James 3) We are accountable for every idle word that proceeds out of our mouths. (Matthew 12:36) Either Christ is Lord of all or not Lord at all. Are we willing to let Him control our tongues?

Today as we consider this verse in Proverbs 29 let us journey through the Word of God to see what God has to say about exercising self-control when it comes to our mouths.

→ Proverbs 17:28 Even a fool is counted wise when he holds his peace: when he shuts his lips, he is considered perceptive.
→ Proverbs 29:20 Do you see a man hasty in his words? There is more hope for a fool than for him.
→ Proverbs 12:18 There is one who speaks like the piercing of a sword, But the tongue of the wise promotes health.
→ Proverbs 10:19 In the multitude of words sin is not lacking. But he who restrains his lips is wise.
→ Proverbs 13:3 He who guards his mouth preserves his life, But he who opens wide his lips shall have destruction.
→ Proverbs 21:23 Whoever guards his mouth and tongue keeps his soul from trouble.
→ Psalm 141:3 Set a guard, O Lord, over my mouth; Keep watch over the door of my lips.
→ Matthew 12:36 But I say to you that for every idle word men may speak, they will give an account of it in the Day of Judgment.
→ Proverbs 15:28 The heart of the righteous studies how to answer, But the mouth of the wicked pours forth evil.
→ Proverbs 18:6 A fools lips enter into contention, And his mouth calls for blows.
→ Proverbs 18:7 A fools mouth is his destruction, And his lips are a snare to his soul.

REFLECTION:

1. When it comes to your mouth, do you by God's grace exercise self-control?

2. If not, why not? Do you recognize the sinful nature of the tongue and its destruction? (James 3:1-12)

3. Do you allow what others say or do to you control what comes out of your mouth?

4. Many hide behind saying things like "I keep it real" or "that's who I am" when it comes to what comes out of their mouth. However, according to this verse it is okay to vent your feelings as long as it's not offensive but the choice to vent all of your feelings it is very clear that it's foolish. It's wise to hold back those things that later you will have to apologize for any way. List some steps that you will begin to take that will prevent you from responding foolishly to others.

5. Begin to develop a habit of exercising self control when it comes to your mouth. This week begin to journal circumstances you are faced with that require you to exercise self control when it comes to your mouth.

6. Share with a friend your desire to change and allow them to hold you accountable. Choose to share with them weekly your victories and struggles in this area.

TEA:

As you explore today's Proverb, take it all in while sipping on a cup of **Pu-erh Tea**. Some of the great benefits of **Pu-erh Tea** are:

→ Reduces cholesterol
→ It cleanses
→ Aids in digestion
→ Aids in weight loss
→ Reduces stress
→ Helps with sleep
→ It has anti-oxidant properties

enJOY!

BE A GIVER

Verse 15 NKJV The leech has two daughters give and give.

The message - A leech has twin daughters named gimme and gimme more.

When I look at the Word of God, the antithesis of gimme and gimme more exists in Philippians 2:3,4 . Nothing that we have belongs to us. It all belongs to God. God created us so that we would reflect Him. He is the ultimate giver. The expectation is that we are giving of ourselves, our time, our resources and our talents.

We live in a very self-absorbed society which is why as Christians we need to focus on doing the very opposite of today's scripture. Don't be a leech. In other words don't be a taker. In a society of taker be intentional about giving!

Today let's take a look at some scriptures that address giving.

Romans 12:1 I beseech you therefore, brethren, by the mercies of God, that you present your bodies a living sacrifice, holy, acceptable to God, which is your reasonable service.

Matthew 6:1-4 Take heed that you do not do your charitable deeds before men, to be seen by them. Otherwise you have no reward from your Father in heaven. Therefore, when you do a charitable deed, do not sound a trumpet before you as the hypocrites do in the synagogues and in the streets, that they may have glory from men. Assuredly I say to you, they have their reward. But when you do a charitable deed, do not let your left hand know what your right hand is doing, that you Father who sees in secret will Himself reward you openly.

Proverbs 22:9 He who has a generous eye will be blessed, For he gives of his bread to the poor.

Proverbs 11:24 There is one who scatters, yet increases more; And there is one who withholds more than is right, But it leads to poverty.

Proverbs 11:25 The generous soul will be made rich, And he who waters will also be watered himself.

Proverbs 28:27 He who gives to the poor will not lack, But he who hides his eyes will have many curses.

James 2: 15,16 If a brother or sister is naked and destitute of daily food, and one of you say depart in peace, be warmed and filled, but you do not give them the things which are needed for the body, what does it profit?

Luke 6:38 Give, and it will be given to you: good measure, pressed down, shaken together, and running over will be put into your bosom. For the same measure that you use, it will be measured back to you.

Luke 6:30 Give to everyone who asks of you. And from him who takes away your goods do not ask them back.

Acts 20:35 ....It is more blessed to give than to receive.

REFLECTIONS:

1. How did today's scriptures speak to you?
2. Be honest with God, are you more like the leech described in Proverbs 30:15 or are you a giver?
3. Do you need to do better at being a giver?
4. Are you intentional about giving?
5. Today ask the Lord to show you opportunities to give.

TEA:

As you explore today's Proverb, take it all in while sipping on a cup of **Dandelion Root Tea**. Some of the great benefits of drinking **Dandelion Root Tea** are:

→ It reduces water weight
→ It can promote liver health.
→ Dandelion tea might sooth digestion ailments.
→ It may help prevent urinary tract infections.
→ It can serve as a laxative.
→ It can help fight diabetes.

enJOY!

BLESSING HIM DAILY!

Verse 12 *She does him good and not evil all the days of her life.*

Amplified version She comforts, encourages, and does him only good as long as there is life within her.

In order to change the climate of your home and change the dynamics of your relationship this verse has to be applied daily. As women we have to be intentional about doing what the scripture encourages even when he's not doing what we think he should be. We are accountable to God and He honors our faith as we make a decision to do what His word says in spite of. Men are wired in such a way that they need continuous encouragement.

If you really want your marriage to thrive, I encourage you to do him good and not evil all the day of your life.

Today let's look at some scriptures that can help us become better and more consistent at "doing good."

Genesis 4:7 If you do well will you not be accepted? And if you do not do well, sin lies at the door. And its desire is for you, but you should rule over it.

Galatians 6:9 And let us not grow weary while doing good, for in due season we shall reap if we do not lose heart.

Colossians 3:17 And whatever you do in word or deed, do all in the name of the Lord Jesus, giving thanks to God the Father through Him.

Colossians 3:23 And whatever you do, do it heartily, as to the Lord and not to men.

James 4:17 Therefore, to him who knows to do good and does not do it, to him it is sin.

III John 1:11 Beloved, do not imitate what is evil, but what is good. He who does good is of God, but he who does evil has not seen God.

Ephesians 2:10 For we are His workmanship, created in Christ Jesus for good works, which God prepared beforehand that we should walk in them.

Galatians 6:10 Therefore, as we have opportunity, let us do good to all, especially to those who are the household of faith.

II Thessalonians 3:13 But as for you, brethren, do not grow weary in doing good.

So, let us not grow weary in well doing for we will reap if we do not faint.

REFLECTIONS:

1. Would you call yourself a Proverbs 31 woman? If so, what makes you a Proverbs 31 woman?
2. If your husband were asked about how you apply this verse how would he answer? Let's be honest. Why do you think he would answer that way?
3. This week think about how you can be more intentional about "doing him good and not evil" and then do it.
4. In this current season in which ways do you think your husband needs more encouragement? Do it!
5. Do you think obedience has anything to do with feelings? Why do you think this question is being asked as it pertains to this verse in Proverbs 31?

TEA:

As you explore today's Proverb, take it all in while sipping on a cup of **Ginkgo leaf Tea**. Some of the great benefits of **Ginkgo leaf Tea** are:

→ Used for memory disorders
→ Can help stimulate and enhance blood circulation of the body.
→ Helps with depression and mood swings
→ It's an antioxidant
→ Prevents and treats strokes

enJOY!

1. Evelyn (02/26/2013). Blackberry leaf. retrieved from http://www.sacredhabits.com/2013/02/26/herb-profile-blackberry-leaf/

2. WebMD (2009). Oolong Tea and its effectiveness. Retrieved from http://www.webmd.com/vitamins-supplements/ingredient-mon-1099-oolong%20tea.aspx?activeingredientid=1099/

3. Jessica Lewis (May 7, 2015). Blueberry Tea Benefits. Retrieved from http://www.livestrong.com/article/24647-blueberry-tea-benefits/

4. Clara Conlon. 11 Benefits of Green Tea that you didn't know about. Retrieved from http://www.lifehach.org/articles/lifestyle/11-benefits-of-green-tea-that-you-didn't-know-about.html

5. RaviTeja and Tanya (March 22,2017). 17 Proven White tea benefits that will surprise you. Retrieved from http://www.stylecraze.com/articles/amazing-benefits-of-white-tea-on0your-health/#gref

6. Cynthia Sass, MPH, RD (March 27,2015). 7 Things you should know about Matcha. Retrieved from http://www.health.com/nutirtion/what-is-matcha

7. Jon Yanoff, CNP (August 2, 2015).10 Surprising Health Benefits of Hisbiscus Tea. Retrieved from http://www.doctorshealthpress.com/food-and-nutrition-articles/hisbiscus-tea-benefits

8. Dena Schmidt (December 7, 2016). Lemongrass tea shown to have great health benefits. Retrieved from http://www.naturalhealth365.com/lemon-grass-tea-2016.html

9. Arshi (June 24, 2016). 11 Amazing Benefits of Rose Hips. http://www.stylecraze.com/articles/amazing-health-benefits-of-rosehips/#gref

10. Bambu. 22 Health Benefits of Ginger root and Ginger Tea. Retrieved from http://www.bambu.com/ginger-benefits/

11. Jeremiah Say (March 2, 2015). 12 Delicious Health Benefits of Cinnamon Tea- Reasons why Cinnamon Tea are extremely vital to your Health. Retrieved from http://www.servingjoy.com/health-benefits-of-cinnamon-tea

12. Tracey Roizman, D.C. (June 19,2015). Papaya Leaf Tea Benefits. Retrieved from http://www.livestrong.com

13. Back to Nature (November 17, 2016). Benefits of Cranberry Tea. Retrieved from http://inetarticle.com/health-benefits-of-cranberry-tea/

14. Dr. Michael Kessler, D.C. (February 23, 2016). 10 Amazing Health Benefits of Peppermint Tea. Retrieved from http://www.doctorshealthpress.com/general-health-articles/health-benefits-of-peppermint-tea

15. Sandi Busch (August 24, 2014). Health Benefits of Pomegranate Tea. Retrieved from http://www.livestrong.com/article/100706-health-benefits-pomegranate-tea/

16. Christina Sarich (July 29, 2013). 29 Nettle Tea Benefits: Sipping on Nettle Tea for Better Health. Retrieved from http://www.naturalsociety.com/29-nettle-tea-benefits-health-herb

17. Dr. Richard Foxx, MD. (May 24, 2016). 8 Powerful Lavender Tea Benefits. Retrieved from http://www.doctorshealthpress.com/general-health-articles/lavender-tea

18. Dr. Edward Group DC, NP, DCBCN, DABFM (January 12, 2015). 9 Impressive Health Benefits of Lemon Balm. Retrieved from http://www.globalhealingcenter.com/natural-health/9-benefits-of-lemon-balm/

19. Sitaranikhil (February 14,2017). 14 Amazing Benefits of Cardamom Tea for Skin, Hair and Health. Retrieved from http://www.stylecraze.com/articles/benefits-of-cardamom-tea-for-skin-hair-and-health/#gref

20. Dr. Josh Axe. 7 Milk Thistle Benefits. Retrieved from http://www.draxe.com/milk-thistle-benefits

21. Sierra Bright (October 28, 2015). 16 Reasons why you should drink Echinacea Tea everyday. Retrieved from https://www.naturallivingideas.com/Echinacea-tea-benefits

22. Anna (February 10, 2016). Blackberry Leaves: Check out their Health Benefits. Retrieved from https://www.green-talk.com/blackberry-leaves/

23. Tara Carson (June 27, 2015). Health Benefits of Hawthorn Tea. Retrieved from https://www.livestring.com/article/285852-health-benefits-of-hawthorn-tea/

24. Deane Alban. 10 Health Benefits of Yerba Mate Tea. Retrieved from https://bebrainfit.com/yerba-mate-benefits/

25. Andrea Macoveiciuc (November 26, 2013). 12 Amazing Health Benefits of Acai Berry Tea. Retrieved from https://www.rivertea.com/blog/12-amazing-health-benefits-of-acai-berry-tea/

26. Dr. Paul Haider (May 23, 2016). 20 Health Benefits of Blueberry leaves. Retrieved from https://shatteringthematrix.com/profile/blogs/20-health-benefits-of-blueberry-leaves#.wo_RvWnyupo

27. Susan Kaye (December 18, 2013). Health Benefits of Red Raspberry Tea. Retrieved from https://www.livestrong.com/article176498-health-benefits-red-rasberry-tea/

28. Vibha Dhawan. 11 Benefits of Black Tea that you didn't know about. Retrieved from https://www.lifehack.org/articles/lifestyle/11-benefits-black-tea.html

29. Aimable Johnson. 9 Proven Health Benefits of Rooibos Tea. Retrieved from https://www.vegkitchen.com/nutition/9-proven-benefits-of-rooibos-tea

30. Jeremiah Say (March 10,2015). Amazing Health Benefits of Pu-erh Tea- 6 Reasons why Pu-erh Tea is extremely good for your body. Retrieved from https://www.servingjoy.com/health-benefits-of-pu-erh-tea/

31. Mia Uren (December 17, 2012). 8 Reasons to drink Dandelion Root Tea. Retrieved from https://www.mindbodygreen.com/0-713418-reasons-to-drink-dandelion-root-tea.html

32. Dr. Axe. How Ginkgo Biloba Benefits Brain Function, Energy and Fights Inflammation. Retrieved from https;//www.draxe.com/ginkgo-biloba-benefits/

Made in the USA
Lexington, KY
19 September 2018